Skittledog

# HOW TO USE THIS JOURNAL

Read the prompts, then paste something over them.

# ABOUT ME

Fill this space with
things you like,
do, own, think...

Poids K^{os}
Gr

Poids Kos
Prix

Write, draw, cut
out and stick down
whatever's on your mind
(big and small).

MUSCLES OF THE EYELID

MUSCLES OF THE EAR

MUSCLES OF EXPRESSION

MUSCLES OF HEAD

MUSCLES OF THE NECK

MUSCLES OF THE SHOULDER BLADE

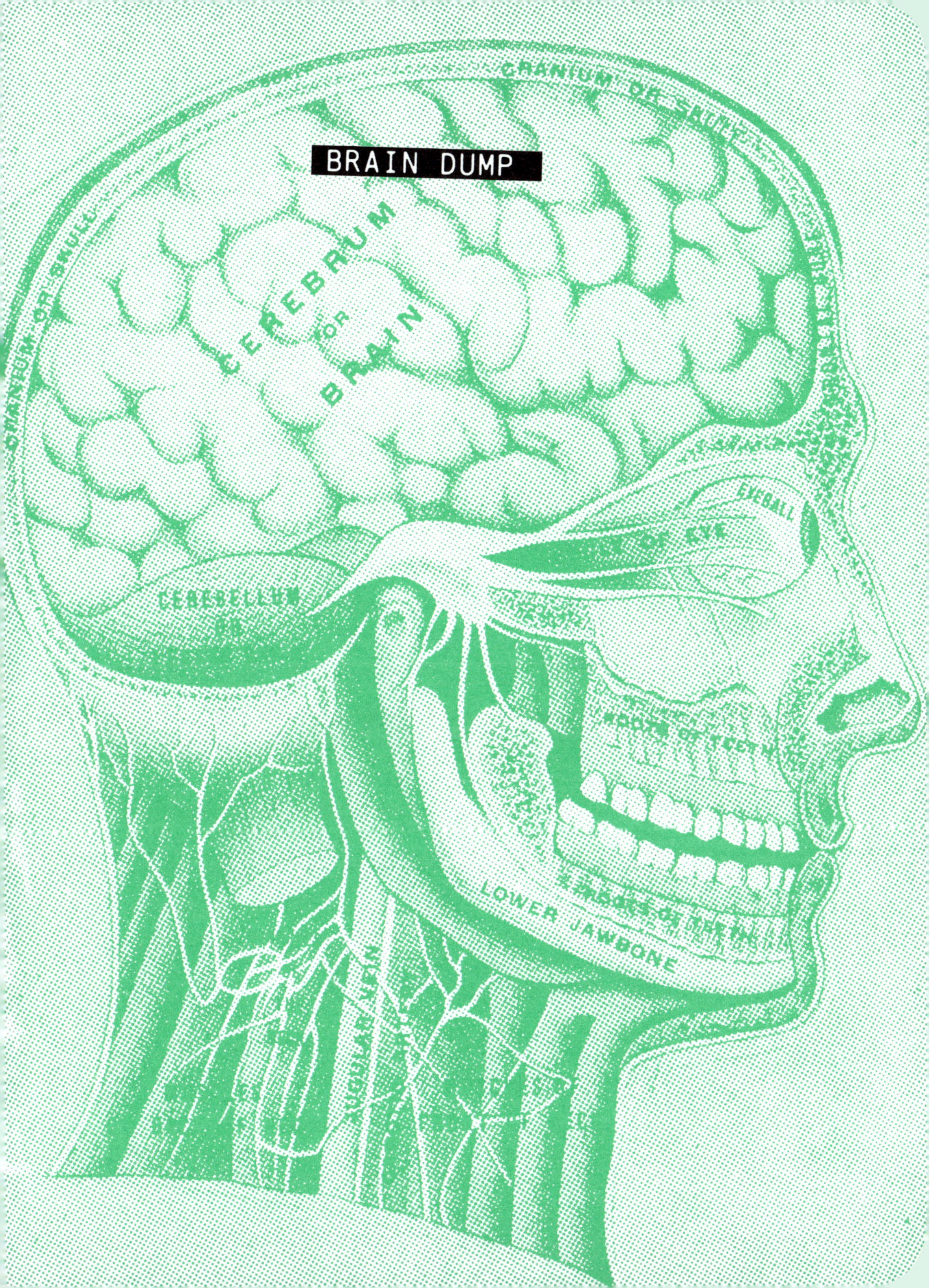
BRAIN DUMP
CRANIUM OR SKULL
CEREBRUM
OR
BRAIN
CEREBELLUM
EYEBALL
ROOTS OF TEETH
LOWER JAWBONE
JUGULAR VEIN

FUTURE ME

Fill this with
your dreams
and aspirations.

Begonia Vernon.

**EGONIA.** See greenhouse plants. One of the fibrous-rooted begonias to use for bedding pur-s, as an annual, is the following:

**ernon.** Handsome leaves, stiff and glossy, of a metallic green color, spotted and margined with azy purple, changing to a dark red as the age of the age advances. Flowers of a brilliant orange carmine, with a bright yellow centre. It blooms freely the entire summer from seed planted in the early spring. Comes true from seed. Greatly admired. Packet, 10 cents.

**BELLIS.** See Daisy.

**BRACHYCOME.** Swan River Daisy. A compact, pretty annual, growing about 8 inches high, and flowering freely during the summer. Flowers blue or white. Sow seed in the open ground, after the weather is warm, or start in boxes or frames and transplant. An excellent flower for cutting. See illustration.

**Mixed.** Pkt., 5 cts.

Brachycome.

**ROWALLIA.** Amethyst. A very handsome ual about eighteen inches high, completly covered ng the summer with blue or white flowers. One of best of bedding plants, and equally satisfactory for low culture. See illustration. Mixed. Pkt., 5 cts.

**USH VERBENA.** Much like the common en favorite in meriterious points, but of compact ead of spraw- g habit of wth. Unique desirable. ket, 15 cents.

**UTTER- Y FLOW-.** *Schizanthus.* behavior of splendid an- at my Briar t trial grounds ants me in king of it in highest terms. ombines ele- e of growth a profusion harmingly ged flowers, of and varied s. It reaches t eighteen inches in height, and the mixture I offer races many types. A single row at Briar Crest pro- d thousands and tens of thousands of blossoms, ing not only profusely but continuously. The col- re purple, white and rose, and the floral markings tints are beautiful. The flower is well named, being butterfly-like in appearance. Pkt., 5 cts.

Browallia.

**CACALIA.** Tassel Flower or Flora's Paint Brush. Summer flowering annual, prized for cutting; 18 inches. Bright scarlet; also yellow. Mixed. Packet, 5 cts.

**CALANDRINIA.** Dwarf annual with large rose colored flowers. Very pretty;

Good winter bloomers, as they do not require much heat. Of the easiest culture.

# SPRING

...ellow. Pkt, 5c.; oz., 20c. ...des of yellow and brown. ...nts.

**CALIFORNIA BELLFLOWER.** See Abutilon.

**CALIFORNIA POPPY.** See Eschscholtzia.

**CALLIRHOE.** Poppy Mallow. This makes a very showy plant for borders and in masses. The blooms are bright red, very profuse and are suitable for bouquets. This plant enjoys a light rich soil and an open sunny position.

**Mixed Varieties.** Packet, 5 cents.

**CALLIOPSIS.** A showy annual formerly classed under the name of Coreopsis, which see. The Calliopsis is half hardy, but not perennial. It makes a quick growth, and produces beautiful foliage. It is one of our brightest and best summer bloomers. Gold and maroon of the most brilliant hues are the prevailing colors. The seeds should be sown in early spring, where the plants are to remain. Thin to six inches.

**Golden Glory.** A new and large type, with flowers on large stems. A continuous and prolific bloomer. Plants a perfect glory of large golden blossoms, double the size of the older sorts. Flowers prettily toothed at the edges. Packet, 10 cts.

**Dwarf Compact.** A new and desirable dwarf strain. Several shades of color. Packet, 5 cents; ounce, 30 cents.

**Fine Mixed.** All the best types. Pkt., 5c.

Callirhoe.

**CANDYTUFT.** See novelties. A beautiful and useful plant of the easiest culture, suitable for the border or garden. The white varieties are extensively grown by florists for bouquets. It flourishes best in cool, moist situations. Sow early in spring and again in August. Height, 1 foot. Thin to stand 6 inches apart. This flower makes a beautiful display every year at my Briar Crest grounds.

**White Rocket.** Large trusses. Pkt., 5c.; oz., 15c.

**Large Flowering Hybrids.** Very dwarf. Nine inches high. Packet, 10 cents; ounce, 25 cents.

**CAPE MARIGOLD.** See Calendula.

**CANNA.** Indian Shot Plant. Stately and highly ornamental foliage plants, from 3 to 5 feet high, suitable for growing singly or in masses. Leaves light green or of a brownish red color. Flowers scarlet and yellow, and very showy. Soak the seed well in warm water before sowing it, or cut with a knife. Take up the roots before freezing weather and preserve in a room or warm cellar. Cannas do best in rich soil, and grow most rapidly in warm weather. For roots see another page of this catalogue. They can be easily grown from seed.

Calendula.

Birdsong, blooms and brighter days. Collage your ultimate spring moments.

Calliopsis, Golden Glory.

**CASTOR OIL BEAN.** *Ricinus.* See noveltie

**CELOSIA.** Cockscomb. This beautiful plant of easiest culture, and is one of the most showy of t summer and autumn bloomers. The minute flow are borne in great masses of various shapes, from th of a cock's comb to that of a feather or plume. T colors are brilliant and striking, from the most viv crimson to the richest orange. Start seeds under gla to hasten bloom; otherwise in the open ground. Gi plenty of room to each plant. Blooming will contin until freezing weather.

**Cristata.** The cock's comb type. Mixed. Packet, 5 cents.

**Plumosa.** The plumed or feathered type. Mixed. Pkt., 5c.

**CENTAUREA.** Sweet Sultans. See Novelties.

**CENTAUREA.** *Centaurea cyanus.* Cyanus, Corn Flower, Ragged Sailor, Blue Bottle. An old garden favorite everywhere, and especially with our German population. It grows in any situation, and blooms freely. Used largely for cut flowers. A variety of colors, including blue, rose and white. (See perennials.)

**Cyanus Minor.** Mixed. Pkt, 5c.; oz., 30c.

**Cyanus Double.** Globular heads. Mixe Many pretty colors. Packet, 10 cents.

Celosia, Plumosa.

**CHRYSANTHEMUM.** French M guerite. Showy and festive garden fav ites, extensively grow for cut flowers. T perennial varieties clude the so-call French Marguerit and Painted Daisi (See perennials. Al see novelties.) The f lowing are annuals:

**Coronarium.** F est double mixe Packet, 5 cents.

**New Double Fringed Hybrid** The large, regular formed, double flowe appear in all colors a shades, including whi yellow, rose, blood r and purple, many them with dark centr bordered with pu white. The foliage dense and gracef Packet, 10 cents.

**Single Fine Mixed.** These ma a beautiful display. T daisy like flowers a handsomely marke usually in bands rings of many colors. Packet, 5 cents; ounce, 30 cent

Caryopteris, Blue Spirea.

**Single and Double Mixed.** This embrac all the standard and new sorts of both single and do ble varieties. Much pleasure may be had the whe summer and fall by the numerous and varied blooms to be had from this gorgeous mixture. Pkt., 10 cents.

**CLEOME.** *Cleome pungens* Giant Spider Plant. A showy annual, four to five feet high, with rose colored flowers

**PRIMULA.** Primrose. Cowslip. Favorite early ...mers of highest merit. For the Chinese primroses ...greenhouse plants on another page. The primula group also includes Auricula and Polyanthus. Culture not difficult. Sow seeds indoors or under glass, and transplant to shaded situations, in rich soil.

Primula Auricula.

**Primula Veris.** Cowslip. Fine mixed. Packet, 5 cents.

**Primula Vulgaris.** True English Primrose. Yellow. Popular. Also called Polyanthus. Pkt., 5c.

**Primula Auricula.** Fragrant. Many rich colors. A hardy primrose, blooming early and often in summer. Packet, 5 cents.

**PYRETHRUM.** Golden Feather. ...dy with daisy-like or aster-like flowers, of several ...rs. Seeds may be started under glass or in the ...ground. In either case the flowers will probably ...ner the second season than the first. About two ... high. Flowers ...e or four inches ...ss, of bright col... including red, ..., white, etc. They ...m during a long ...od.

**...ngle Hybrid.** ...ed colors. Packet, ...ents.

**...olden Feather.** ...wn for its yellow ...ge; 6 to 9 inches ... Packet, 10 cts.

**...oseum.** Persian ...ct powder plant. ... insect powder is ...le from the flowers, ...ch are dried after ...pollen has formed. ...ket, 10 cents.

**...OSE SEED.** See ...le Midget or Baby ...es in novelties.

Pyrethrum.

Sweet Rocket.

**SWEET ROCKET.** Hardy perennials bearing purple or white flowers. Plants two or three feet high. Flowers fragrant. A rich, light soil is required, and the plants should be moved after blooming. Double fine mixed. Packet, 5 cents.

**STEVIA.** See greenhouse plants.

**SWEET WILLIAM.** *Dianthus barbatus.* A well-known, free-flowering plant which has been greatly improved of late years. It produces masses of lovely, brilliant blossoms through a long period. It makes a splendid effect in beds. The colors are rich and varied. The plant is perfectly hardy, and comes up with increased vigor year by year.

**Fine Double Mixed.** A splendid strain of sweet william; all colors. Packet, 5 cents.

**Fine Single Mixed.** Various beautiful shades and markings. Pkt., 5 cts.

**Auricula Flowered Perfection.** A handsome class, each flower having a clearly defined eye. Mixed colors. Pkt., 5 cts.

**Mammoth Holborn Glory.** A beautiful new strain with large flowers and bushy compact habit of growth. Single florets have measured over one inch across. Embraces many shades and markings. 2½ ft. high. Pkt., 10c.

Sweet William.

Viola, The Czar.

**TRITOMA.** ... Hot Poker. Torch Flower. Hardy perennial plant, producing tall spikes of orange red flowers; three to four feet. Blooms from August until late autumn. Very showy and striking in beds or masses.

**Uvaria.** Varies from yellow to scarlet. Packet, 5 cents.

**VALERIANA.** Hardy heliotrope. A showy border plant producing large corymbs of beautiful flowers suitable for bouquets or decorations. Very fragrant, resembling heliotrope. Two to three feet. Should be largely grown, as it succeeds almost everywhere. A desirable perennial.

**Mixed.** Rose, red and white. Packet, 5 cents.

**VIOLA.** Violet. The popular sweet violet. It blooms very early in the spring. It is perfectly hardy, but repays winter protection, coming earlier. The violet can easily be grown from seed.

**The Czar.** Rich blue. Very large flowering. Packet, 10 cents.

**Fine Mixed.** All the new and old varieties. Packet, 10 cents.

**WALLFLOWER.** A hardy or half-hardy perennial bearing long spikes of exquisitely fragrant flowers. It is very ornamental in the border or in forming groups. Blooms in spring. Sow thinly in shallow drills in early spring. When well started transplant to twelve inches apart.

**Double Mixed.** About twelve colors. Packet, 10 cents.

**Single Mixed.** Fine mixture. Very desirable. Packet, 5 cts.

Double Wallflower.

# EVERLASTINGS, ORNAMENTAL GRASSES AND AQUATICS.

## EVERLASTINGS.

The so-called everlasting flowers get their name from the peculiar character of their rays or petals. They are justly popular, not only for their summer display in the garden, but because they will retain their beauty for years, if cut as soon as they come into full bloom, tied in small bunches and allowed to dry slowly in the shade, with the heads downward to keep the stems straight. I offer the best everlastings that are known.

Globe Amaranth.

**ACROCLINIUM.** Graceful annual border plants, one foot high. Valuable for winter bouquets and decorations. Finest mixed rose and white. Pkt., 5 cts.

**AMMOBIUM.** A pretty and useful little white flower for bouquets. Stiff and angular in appearance; hardy annual; eighteen inches.

**Alatum Grandi...rum.** The largest flowering sort, produces an ...rmous crop of pure white flowers. Packet, 5 cents.

**...ACHELOR'S BUTTON.** See Globe Ama...th. Also known as Gomphrena.

**...LOBE AMARANTH.** Bachelor's Button. A ...der annual. Seeds rather slow to germinate, and ...uld be started early, in window box or hot bed and ...nsplanted. Colors white, purple, striped, etc. Un... good treatment a single plant will produce several ...dred flowers. The flowers should be cut just before ...y are fully ripe, for the best permanent bouquets. ...y pretty. About two feet high.

**...ana Compacta.** ...ed. Only a few inches ...h. A mass of bloom. ...ket, 5 cents.

**...ixed Colors.** All the ...colors. Packet, 5 cts.

**...ELICHRYSUM.** ...aw Flower. Large, full ...ble flowers, of various ...ors, from white and ...ght yellow to scarlet, ...ded and tipped. Exceed...ly handsome bouquets ...winter. Annual. Easy ...ure. Two feet or less.

**...warf Double**

Gynerium. (Pampas Grass.)

Rhodanthe.

**RHODANTHE.** A very pretty annual, about one foot high, belonging to the everlasting group. Flowers white, pink, crimson, etc. Select light, rich soil, in a sheltered situation. Seeds require careful starting, but the bloom well repays all trouble. Flowers bell-shaped; beautiful when dried. Suitable for pot culture. Finest mixed, embracing all the best and most prolific varieties. Packet, 5 cents.

**STRAW FLOWER.** See Helichrysum.

**XERANTHEMUM.** Beautiful, free-blooming annual, one foot high, highly prized as an everlasting. Large, double, globe-shaped flowers. Seeds germinate easily in open ground. Set ten inches apart. Fine mixed; all colors. Pkt., 5 cts.

**FINEST MIXED EVERLASTINGS.** All the leading varieties in a single packet. Packet, 10 cents.

## ORNAMENTAL GRASSES.

The ornamental grasses are indispensable for garden or lawn, being beautiful and graceful in summer, in the green state, and equally desirable when dried for interior decoration during the winter season. I offer a few of the best.

**EULALIA. Japonica Zebrina.** Zebra Grass. A robust perennial grass from Japan, forming handsome clumps. Six feet. Hardy. Beautiful plumes. Leaves variegated; crosswise bars. Pkt., 10c.

**GYNERIUM. Argenteum.** Pampas Grass. Half hardy perennial, a native of South America. Very beautiful. Roots require winter protection, or to be lifted and kept in greenhouse or cellar. Taller than Eulalia. Gynerium blooms the second season from seed, and its white, silvery plumes well repay

**JOB'S TEARS.** *Coix Lachryma.* Broad leaves and hard, shining seeds of peculiar appearance, giving the plant its name. Annual. Two feet. Packet, 5 cents.

**PAMPAS GRASS.** See Gynerium Argenteum.

**PURPLE FEATHER GRASS.** Beautiful and already popular. See novelties.

**ZEBRA GRASS.** See Eulalia Japonica.

**ORNAMENTAL GRASSES. Mixed.** Embracing many varieties of ornamental grasses additional to those listed. Packet, 10 cts.; ounce, 25 cts.

## AQUATICS.

It is quite possible to raise water lilies from seeds; and the greater the care the greater the reward. People having control of shallow ponds, access to streams or rivers, may well experiment in this direction. Small artificial ponds or pools can be constructed for the purpose, or tanks can be made of wood. Half barrels filled with water will answer very well for summer, but permanent operations are most successful where the frost cannot exercise a hostile effect. Many of the water lilies are perfectly hardy, and are not hurt by the winter, and it is only necessary to establish them in order to enjoy a wealth of beautiful and fragrant blossoms year after year. Some of the water lilies produce floating flowers; others raise the bloom quite into the air. The flower colors run through a wide range, including white, pink, blue, yellow, etc., with rich fragrance. In general terms it is only needful to plant the seeds in rich soil, in pans or boxes, and to cover this rich soil with sand (to hold the soil in place), and then to sink the pan or box in shallow water. Cow manure and earth (the former well rotted) make a good medium for the growth of the lily roots.

**NELUMBIUM. Luteum.** American Lotos. Hardy. Pkt., 15c.

# LYRICS

Fill this
with the
song lyrics
that live in
your head.

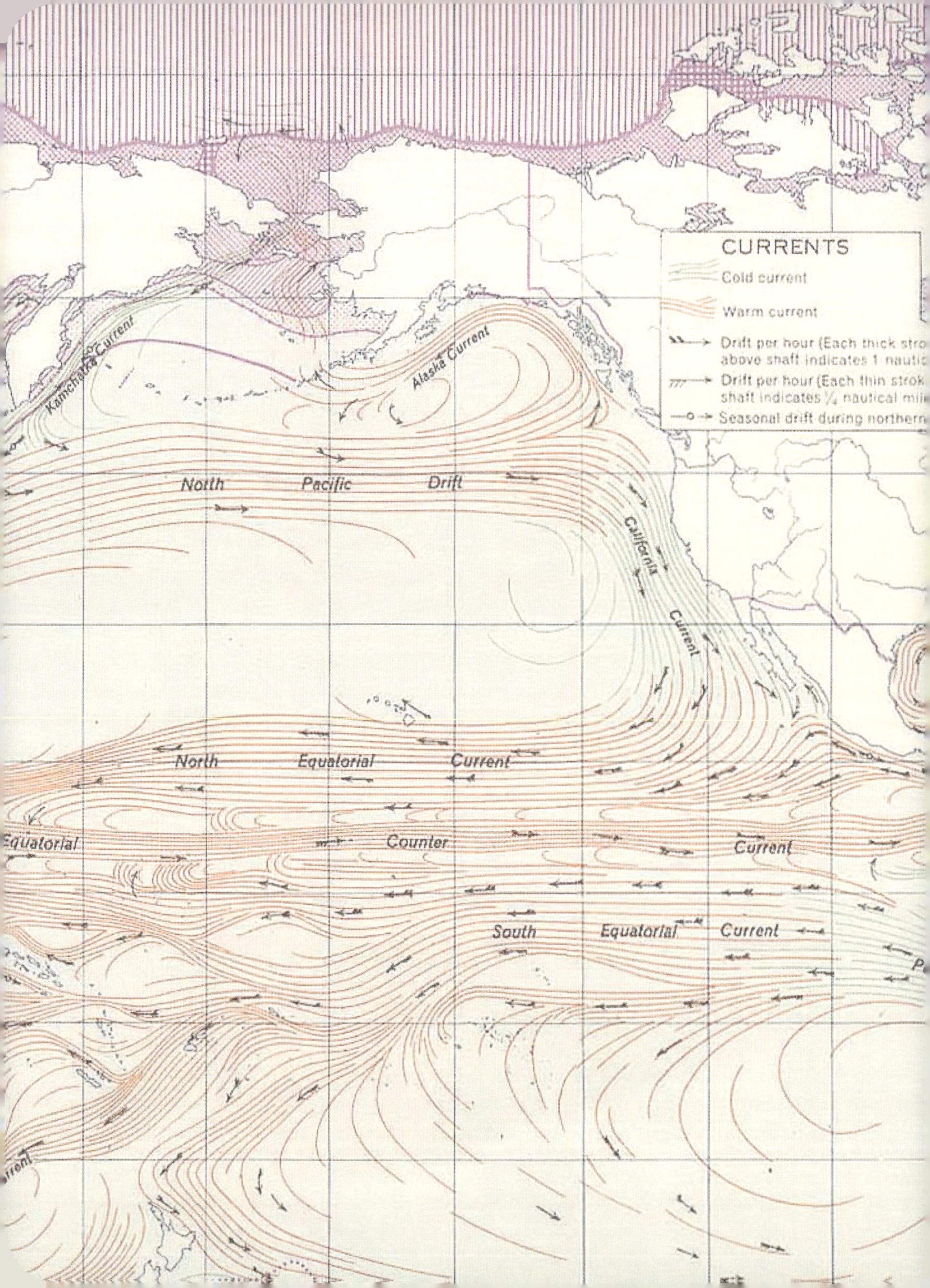
CURRENTS
Cold current
Warm current
Drift per hour (Each thick stro
above shaft indicates 1 nautic
Drift per hour (Each thin strok
shaft indicates ¼ nautical mil
Seasonal drift during northern
Kamchatka Current
Alaska Current
North
Pacific
Drift
California
Current
North
Equatorial
Current
Equatorial
Counter
Current
South
Equatorial
Current

West Greenland Current
East Greenland Current
Current
Cold Wall
Gulf Stream
North
Atlantic
Drift
Rennell Current
Portugal C.
Canary Current
Antilles Current
Caribbean Current
North Equatorial Current
Guinea Current
South Equatorial Current
Brazil Current
Benguela Current

WORDS

Poids K^os
Pr

Poids K^{os}
Prix

Birthday, wedding,
holiday or
festival... Stick
your mementos here.

CELEBRATE

# FRUIT STICKERS

# TRIPS

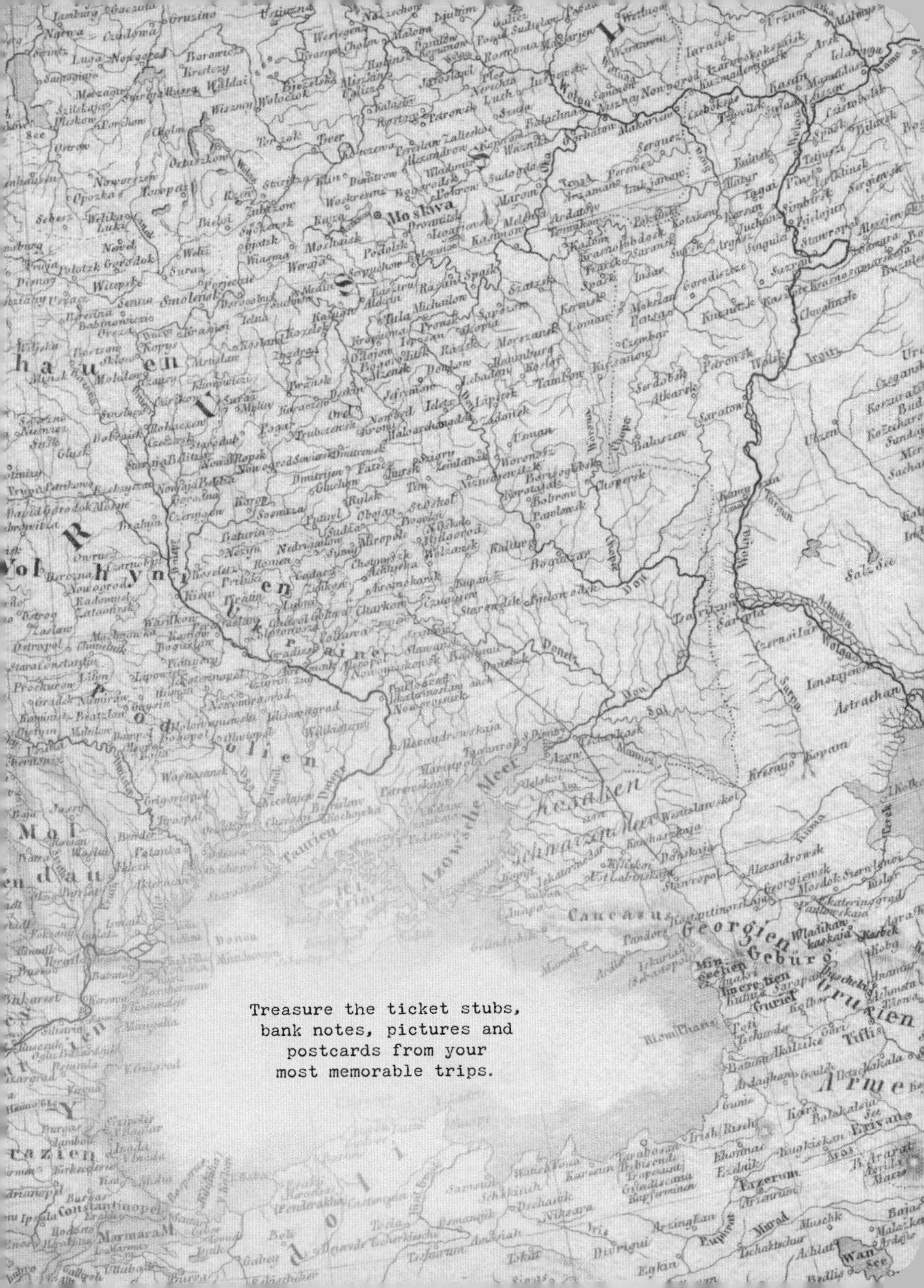


Treasure the ticket stubs, bank notes, pictures and postcards from your most memorable trips.

INS

OUTS

Awaken the senses with perfume samples, dried flowers or even a few drops of your favourite essential oil.

ADD
SCENT

d'Henri BERNARD
ENVOI D
Andantino.
3
mf
Pour vous o_bli_ger de pen_ser à
moi, D'y pen_ser sou vent, d'y pen_ser en_co_re.
Voi_ci quel_ques fleurs, bien modeste en_voi, De très humbles
fleurs qui vien_nent d'é clo re. Ce ne sont pas
rall.
là de no_bles bou_quets Si_gnés de la main de sa_vants fleu_
_ris_tes, Li és par des nœuds de ru_bans co_
_quets, Bouquets pré_ci_eux, chefs-d'œuvre d'ar_tis_tes,
3
Ce sont d'humbles fleurs, pres_que fleurs des
champs Mais ce sont des fleurs sim_ples et sin_cè_res

# FLEURS

Musique de Paul DELMET

Des fleurs sans or - gueil, aux li - bres pen - chants, Des fleurs de po -

- ète à deux sous, pas chè - - - res J'au - rais mieux ai -

- me de ri - ches bi - joux Que ce sou - ve - nir vraiment trop cham -

- pê - tre, Ba - gues, bra - ce - lets, fé - mi - nins jou -

joux, J'au - rais mieux ai - mé .. vous aus - si, peut - ê - - -

tre. Mais du moins ces fleurs, ce mo - deste en - voi, Ces très hum - bles

fleurs qui viennent d'é - clo - re Vous di - ront tout

bas de pen - ser à moi, D'y pen - ser sou -

vent, d'y pen - ser en - co - - re!

# FOOD

Coffee-cup sleeves, menus,
tin-can wrappers, restaurant
receipts... Collect the
paper reminders of all your
favourite foods.

SCREW
IT UP

Scrunch it, fold it,
tear it. We all screw up
now and again - your junk
doesn't need to be stuck
here perfectly.

CURRENT FAVES

# FLAPS, LAYERS & POCKETS

Stick down an
envelope here to
make a pocket.

STICKER DUMP
LA ROSA ESPAÑOLA
S.V.Cª
Fill this spread with stickers only.

BOOKS I'VE READ

COLLECT

Arrange paper bags,
wrapping paper, magazine
pages, cards and ribbons
as you please.

CARTE P

La Correspondance au recto n'est pa

(Se rensei

Partie réservée à la Correspondance

Simone embrasse
Louise, ainsi que
maman et papa.
Bonne fête. (ici
Dimanche)

Emile

OSTALE

Adresse du Destinataire

Madame

Louise Deloir

Hotel de Normandie

16 Rue du Caire

Paris

SUMMER
2
3
1

Beach time,
barbecues, blue
skies. What does
summer say to you?
8
9
10

WISHLIST

# VISION BOARD

BINGO

# BINGO

**Abonamentul :**

Pe un an . . . . . . . 24 lei
» 6 luni . . . . . . . 12 »
» 3 » . . . . . . . 6 »

*Pentru streinătate se adaogă portul.*

NUMERUL 10 BANI

# EVENIM

ZIAR NAȚI

ZIAR QUOTIDIAN

Lunĭ 1 F

## Direcția nóstră politică

*Partidul național-liberal are la activul seu cele mai glorioase acte realizate în această țară.*

*Istoria, dreaptă și nepărtinitoare, a inregistrat toate faptele marĭ săvărșite la noi de liberalĭ și a pus pecetea pe ele, odată pentru totdeauna, spre neschimbare. Decĭ ori-ce trudă, ori-ce încercărĭ și ori-ce tendințĭ din partea vrăjmașilor partidului liberal, fie de-a slăbi insemnătatea neprețuită a actelor indeplinite de eĭ, fie de-a falșifica istoria noastră politică, — toate se sdrobesc în fața realităței care apare senină și nepătată în cugetul curat al omului de omenie.*

*timp, o mare și imediată torie și pe care virtutea c țenească chiar o reclamă.*

*Tendințĭ năprasnice și p culoase apar în maĭ toate tele regimuluĭ conservator c deține astăzĭ puterea. Atât p legiuirele luĭ, cât și prin a le sale pur administrative, dința de a știrbi muma legilo Constituțiunea—resare în i isbitor.*

*Și in contra acesteĭ tend avem o imperioasă datorie a-ne rîdica cu toată tăria veghia apoĭ, în primul loc,* Domnirea Legilor *inscrisă fruntea programuluĭ să primească loviturĭ.*

*Orĭ de căte orĭ conservat 'șĭ vor manifesta tendințĭ a știrbi Constituțiunea, d tăinui abuzurile și jafurile*

IENTUL

NAL-LIBERAL.

Pagina III, linia . . . .
» IV, » . . . . .

Abonamentele lunar
primesc un scădĕmênt
50 la sută.

NUMERUL 10 BA

ruarie 1893

№ 1.

A-se vedea pe pagina III-a ultimele telegrame.

UN MANDAT... ELECTORAL!

—

*Partidul conservator, o știe toată țara, s'a distins pururea prin sistemul seu electoral vițiat de violențe și corupțiune. Când regimul compromis de la 1876 s'a prăbușit, comisiunea de anchetă însărcinată cu cercetările actelor acestuĭ regim, a adunat și publicat într'un volum o serie întreagă de nelegiuirĭ făptuite în timpul perioadelor electorale. Astăzĭ încă, deși sunt aproape două deceniĭ, cetățeniĭ n'au uitat sistemul electoral al conservatorilor*

## SILUETE

—

VASILE POGOR.

Se svonește că are 60 anĭ. El o știe, n'o crede. Îșĭ ingrijește artistic fisicul. rurea zimbitor și grațios. A glumit și mai bine de jumătate veac. Junimist fii că crede că e in partidul zeflemele lor. Fig de paradă, plină de decorațiĭ. N'a făcut ni in politică de și Iașul l'a avut și 'l are primar și deputat. N'a vorbit nicĭ odată tribuna publică. Mulțumește in 25 de cuvi când este ales primar sau vice-președinte Camerei. Are avere mare și primește astă ca și în trecut, diurne și lefurĭ. Astăzĭ e a betat de chestiile marĭ la ordinea zileĭ sfatul comunal. Se observă în el o luptă sine însușĭ. Raiul și Iadul s'au întâlnit fața sa și 'șĭ dispută prioritatea. O ideea m îĭ frămantă cugetul: transformarea pămân rilor comunale în apă potabilă.

Semne particulare: Merge cu un pe metru și vorbește cu.... centimetru.

KIKERIKI

—

DIN ACTELE SECRET

ale

DIPLONAȚIEI RUSE.

Give this page a wash of watercolour, big splodge of ink or get rustic with tea and coffee stains.

PAINT IT
INK IT
STAIN IT

9
WORKING
9 TO 5

Document your working
day, career highlights
or even the best
water-cooler moments.

5

BATHROOM RAID
Perfume labels,
make-up smudges,
skincare routines...
Collage your cosmetics.

CLOSER TO

NATURE

Pressed flowers, bark rubbings, botanical sketches or a map of your favourite walk. Collect your experience of the great outdoors.

# JUNK THE DAY

1

2

3

4

5

6

7

8

9

10

11

12

13

14

15

16

17

18

19

20

21

22

23

24

I WANT
CANDY

A sugar hit AND
a pop of colour.
Stick your
favourite candy
wrappers here.

# PERFECT PLAYLIST

Tracks you'll never
tire of. YOUR ultimate,
curated playlist.

I'M SO
LUCKY

BSS 28

~~LIBRARY~~

10 THINGS I'M GRATEFUL FOR

AUTHOR

TITLE

| BORROWER'S NAME | | DATE DUE |
|---|---|---|
| | | |
| | | |
| | | |
| | | |
| | | |

~~LIBRARY~~

POSITIVE AFFIRMATIONS

AUTHOR

TITLE

| BORROWER'S NAME | | DATE DUE |
|---|---|---|
| | | |
| | | |
| | | |
| | | |
| | | |
| | | |

BSS 28

~~LIBRARY~~

AUTHOR

TITLE

| BORROWER'S NAME | | DATE DUE |
|---|---|---|
| | | |
| | | |
| | | |
| | | |
| | | |
| | | |

~~LIBRARY~~

BSS 28

NOTES OF APPRECIATION

AUTHOR

TITLE

| BORROWER'S NAME | | DATE DUE |
|---|---|---|
| | | |
| | | |
| | | |
| | | |
| | | |
| | | |
| | | |

~~LIBRARY~~

BSS 28

AUTHOR

TITLE

| BORROWER'S NAME | | DATE DUE |
|---|---|---|
| | | |
| | | |
| | | |
| | | |
| | | |
| | | |
| | | |

HOME
SWEET HOME

What's meaningful to you?
Photos of your house,
family recipe cards,
memories of loved ones?
This space is yours to
make homely.

Crunchy leaves,
cinnamon sticks and
pumpkins galore.
What are your autumn
essentials?

GREETINGS

Rescue your most
treasured birthday,
anniversary and
thank you cards
from wherever
they're hiding.

## LIGHTS, CAMERA, ACTION

Tickets, reviews, posters or popcorn boxes. Fill with movie memorabilia from your favourite films.

BEACON THEATRE
Superior Wisconsin
ADMIT ONE
Good This Date Only
20
CENTS
20754

RENE BRUNET THEATRES
ADMIT ONE
0193545
0193545

VINCENT'S
BERWICK, PA.
Keep This Ticket
088442

MY
SECRET
STASH

Stamps, coins,
teenage trading
cards. Pimp this
space with nostalgia
from a forgotten
collection.

PLANETARY
ECLIPSE OF THE SUN.
THE ZODIACAL LIGHT
ARGO NAVIS
CANIS MAJOR
HYDRA
CANCER
COLUMBA
GEMINI
ORION
TAURUS
PERSEUS
CETUS
PISCES
ANDROMEDA
PEGASUS
SCULPTORIS
PISCIS AUSTRALIS

SYSTEM.
THE MOON.
METEORIC SHOWER.
HYDRA
CORVUS
CENTAURUS
VIRGO
SATURN
LUPUS
BOOTES
LIBRA
SCORPIO
DRACO
HERCULES
OPHIUCHUS
LYRA
AQUILA
ANTINOUS
SAGITTARIUS
CAPRICORNUS
EARTH

Print your best
photos and set
them free from
the cloud!
SCRAPBOOK
NOT
SCREENSHOT

Experiment with junk
in just one colour.

TONE

IT DOWN

1
2
3
4
5
6
BLACK AND
WHITE
Make these pages a vision in monochrome.

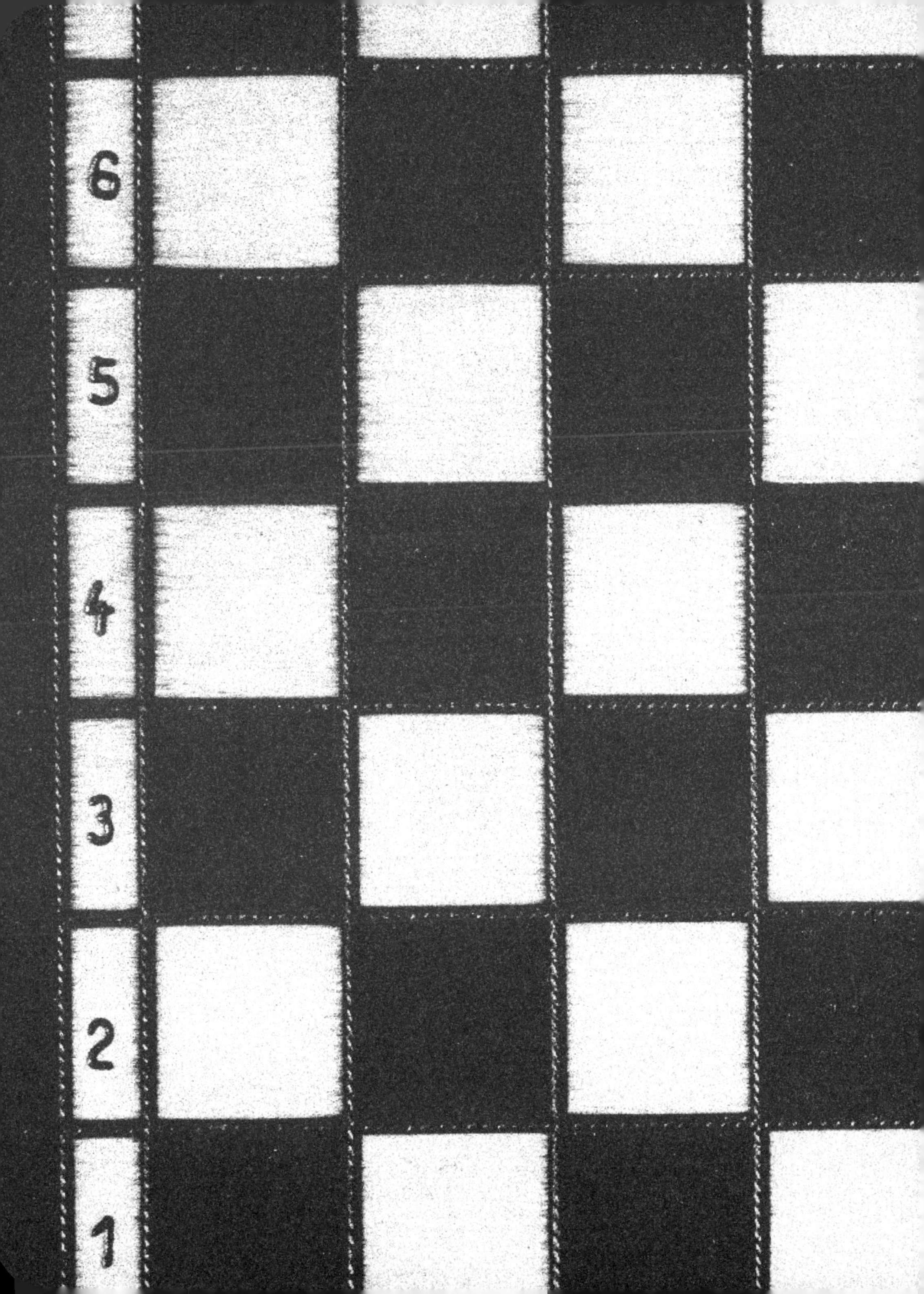
6
5
4
3
2
1

CLOSET COLLAGER

38N8041—Buff.
38N8042—Black.
Size about 24x60 in. excluding fringe.
A luxurious ... very comfortable Shawl-Scarf that one can hardly do without in autumn or winter months. Beautifully knit in the links and links stitch of fine quality all wool worsted yarns. Neatly striped in contrasting colors. Long hand-knotted fringe.

98c

38N8331—Buff.
38N8332—Silver Gray.
Shipping weight, 7 oz.
Becoming Sport Cap that is dressy and warm. Knit from all wool yarn with a beautiful soft Angora finish. Novel wool rosette trims the attractive cuff. The fashioned crown has piped seams in contrasting color.

$1.35

$1.69

Headwear

67c

38N8229—Red combination.
38N8230—Peacock blue combination.
38N8231—Buff combination.
Shipping weight, 7 oz.
Snappy style, close fitting all wool Docker Cap for schoolgirls. Novelty star design, knit in contrasting color, outlined with Rayon. The cuff of double thickness has fancy knit border in colors to match star.

Your visual style edit is here. Find clothing tags, store receipts and shots of your style icons.

SMOKEY

## PET PROFILE

NAME..................................

AGE....................................

LIKES..................................

DISLIKES..............................

DAILY
Stick, write, draw and
document the things
you do to feel good.

DOPAMINE

BFFs

Dedicate this
page to your
best friends.

CHRISTMAS PRIZES ❧ THE E

Wednesday snow.

HT
ON

"Circulation Books Open to All."

T. NEW YORK, TUESDAY, DECE

# HELD ON
# GERY CHARGE

Man Who Was Made y of Aged Woman rlem Taken Into Custion of Fraud.

ained by Assistant Dis- Krotel, and the Prisoner the Tombs to Await a Bondsman.

e was arrested this afternoon on a war- e deeds which purported to dispose of the Harlem miser.

his office, at No. 304 Broadway, with a as arrested by Detective Flood, of the s believed that Alderdice was about to

to the Elizabeth street station, and from for arraignment.

rotel, who has had the Oliver investiga- ate Breen for the warrant.

rant in the belief, based upon a handwrit- ture to various deeds transferring $100,000 erdice was forged.

erdice, through his counsel, George Simp- , entered a plea of not guilty. Assistant at bail be fixed at $5,000, saying that the to forgery in the first degree. Mr. Simp- and a compromise was reached at $3,500. ck was the time set for the examination. to wait the arrival of a bondsman.

Rev. James Alderdice, who lived next

# FAVORITES WIN AT NEW ORLE

## BIG BEN BEATEN BY FRANK BELL

"Doc" Street's Horse Was Heavily Played to Win Second Race at Crescent City, but Is Outsprinted by Winner.

IRENE LINDSEY GETS HOME IN FRONT IN FIRST.

Bountiful Graduates from the Maiden Ranks by Taking the Third Event from Symphony and Trossachs.

THE WINNERS.

FIRST RACE — Irene Lindsey (even) 1, Morning Star (5 to 2) 2, Little Jack Horner 3.

SECOND RACE—Frank Bell (3 to 1) 1, Big Ben (2 to 5) 2. Van Ness 3.

THIRD RACE—Bountiful (3 to 1) 1, Symphony (7 to 2) 2. Trossachs 3.

(Special to The Evening World.)

RACE TRACK, NEW ORLEANS, La., Dec. 8.—The track was still soft in spots to-day.

Another good crowd was out and the speculative element kept the bookmakers busy. Jockey Higgins will be here

# SPECIAL E

## LATE SCO IN CYCLE R AT THE GA

Scores of the leaders at 6 o'clock in th

| | M. | L. | |
|---|---|---|---|
| Leander & Butler.... | 783 | 7 | Walthour |
| Newkirk & Jacobson.. | 783 | 7 | Contenet |
| Bedell Brothers...... | 783 | 7 | Galvin & |
| Root & Doran........ | 783 | 7 | Fl. Krebs |
| Bowler & Fisher...... | 783 | 7 | Keegan |
| Fr. Krebs & Barclay.. | 783 | 3 | Samson |
| Gougoltz & Rettich.... | 783 | 1 | Dove & |

CORBETT MAY AGAIN FIGHT

Jim Corbett, according to report, has to fight Jim Jeffries before a club in the wordl's fair next year. Corbett, who is in accepted the offer. Corbett demands a

LATE RESULTS AT NEW OR

Fourth Race—Witful 1, Ancke 2, Bon

Fifth Race—Siddons 1, Adeante 2, A

Sixth Race—Foresight 1, Rainland 2,

# FLOOD STOPS WO

TUNNEL TO B

ENING WORLD'S PRIZE STORY

N

# World.

# EXTRA

"Circulation Books Open to All."

8, 1903. PRICE ONE CENT.

NS.

RA.

ES
CE
DEN

le race:

| | M. | L. |
|---|---|---|
| roo.. | 783 | 7 |
| on... | 783 | 7 |
| tt... | 783 | 7 |
| erson. | 783 | 7 |
| an...... | 783 | 6 |
| erst't | 783 | 3 |
| th... | 774 | 8 |

EFF.

fered a purse
City during the
it is said, has
eed purse.

tive Girl 3.

IN

## FIVE IN HOME KILLED BY FIRE

**Only One in Entire Family to Escape Flames Was Son Fifteen Years Old, Who Leaped to Safety from Window.**

**MOTHER, BEWILDERED, WOULD NOT THROW BABY.**

**While Neighbors Rushed to Find a Ladder the Unfortunate Woman Toppled Back Into the Flames, Holding the Infant.**

FREEHOLD, N. J., Dec. 8.—One child, a boy of fifteen, is all of the family of Clayton Fowler, of Carksbury, ten miles from here, who escaped from the flames which destroyed the Fowler home early to-day.

Fowler and his wife and three of their children, one of them an infant six months old, were burned to death, and all that remains of their pretty little home is a smouldering pile of ashes.

The dead are Fowler, who was forty-two years old; Elizabeth, his wife, thirty-six years old; Wilhelmina, thirteen years old; Martha, five years, and Willie, six months old. George, the oldest child, who is fifteen, escaped by jumping from a window of the second floor. He landed safely on the ground below, sustaining only slight injuries.

The Fowlers lived in a two-story frame house in the heart of the village. The entire family was asleep when the house caught fire. Fowler was roused by the smell of smoke and discovered that the chimney had caught fire. Not appreciating the danger, he tried to extinguish the flames, instead of rousing his family and getting them to a place of safety.

Within five minutes the entire lower

# FEARFUL STRAIN ON BIKE RACERS CALLS FOR 'DOPE'

**Trainers at Garden Grind Set Out Queer Looking Bottles as Night Approaches—Long Hours of Riding Begins to Tell on the Weary Legged Racers.**

**FASTEST SPRINTING OF THE RACE DURING THE AFTERNOON.**

**Moran, After Last Lap, Keeps Leaders on the Jump All the Time---Experts Pick Leander to Carry Off First Honors---Bedell Not Suffering.**

MADISON SQUARE GARDEN, Dec. 8.—The "dope" bottles will come into play to-night at the big six-day grind.

The fearful strain on the struggling riders is becoming too much for human nature to stand, and the trainers of both the foreign and the American riders are getting out the queer looking bottles that have played such an important part in races of the past.

Up to the present there has not been any use of "dope" to the

WINTER

廣重画

Snowfall, twinkling lights and cups of cocoa. Turn these pages into a winter wonderland.

Skittledog

First published in the United Kingdom in 2026
by Skittledog, an imprint of Thames & Hudson Ltd,
6-24 Britannia Street, London WC1X 9JD


Designer: Alison Guile
Production: Felicity Awdry

With thanks to the Public Domain Review, Unsplash, Pexels and Wikimedia Commons for pictures used to create the backgrounds.



EU Authorized Representative: Interart S.A.R.L.
19 rue Charles Auray, 93500 Pantin, Paris, France
productsafety@thameshudson.co.uk
www.interart.fr

A CIP catalogue record for this book is available from the British Library

ISBN 978-1-83776-108-1
01

Printed and bound in China by C&C Offset Printing Co, Ltd

Be the first to know about our new releases, exclusive content and author events by visiting:

skittledog.com
thamesandhudson.com
thamesandhudsonusa.com
thamesandhudson.com.au